THE WINDOW

An Urban Gardening Primer

A Fascinating Story of Growth

Written by: The Green Neighbor

Introduction

How does one initiate a modest project, such as an urban garden, in an urban setting with its unique constraints? This primer was created to serve as an easy-to-read guide with practical steps to start small and grow exponentially through knowledge in action.

Your Window Awaits

Grow!

Plant the seeds of your garden.

Growth, please!

But why the focus on plants?

An Urban Desert

An urban desert is an area in which it is difficult to buy affordable or good quality fresh food. Planting and growing plants bring life needed to the food desert. This way more people can enjoy the health benefits of having access to fresh, nutritious, healthy foods.

No resume or experience is needed.

Immediate growth opportunity.

Have You Ever Grown Plants Before??

By learning how to grow and tend to plants, you can help combat food deserts and have yummy, nutritious food at your fingertips.

What Do You Want to Grow?

How Will You Decide?

Imagine...

Picking fresh strawberries from your window.

Harvesting

Will you harvest fresh basil leaves for homemade pizza? Or cherry tomatoes to pop on your salad?

What do you already have that you can use to get started?

Let's review a list of things needed for you to begin this exciting journey of growth.

Must-haves For Your Efforts

- Sunlight
- Water
- Seeds
- Containers
- Discipline
- Consistency

What is Important to Know About the Sunlight?

Sunlight is free. Consider the amount and strength of the sunlight that you have in your planting environment. All plants need sunlight to varying degrees.

Southern, sunny, exposure is not a prerequisite. Do a little research. Discover the possibilities. Find plants that will thrive where you are. Remember. There is always room for growth.

Water Is Life

All living things, like plants, animals, and people, need water to live. Different plants need different amounts of water to survive.

So, you must be knowledgeable about the watering requirements of the plant you choose to grow.

Seeds

The Sky Is The Limit

You can find seeds in your food, and you can buy seeds from a florist, or a plant store. Make sure to do your research and ask lots of questions for the most successful growth of your plants.

Containers

Look around before you spend any money.

Do you already have something that you can make use of as a container? You could use an old cast iron pot, old coffee containers, or a reused 5-gallon container. Possibilities are as creative as your ideas! Just think outside the box and look for containers that are made out of simple, natural materials, that can be safely reused.

Discipline

Just like every day, you must do homework, wash, and get dressed. Plan activities with your plant. Take responsibility for providing the things your plant needs to grow.

When it is thirsty it will be counting on you. If the soil is lacking, the plant will need your help to survive and thrive. Come through with water, some attention, and a little tender, loving, thoughtful care on a regular basis. And watch for the growth.

Consistency

Think of your gardening on a schedule. Every day, you need to give your plant friends some attention. Just like giving them a drink when they're thirsty, this also helps them grow strong.

Do all these things regularly. Like how you eat, drink, and take care of yourself every day. Your plant friends will grow strong and happily, thrive, and look amazing. Then, your plants will be able to handle any challenges that come their way, and you will have mastered a new and valuable life skill.

Remember to grow anywhere, everywhere, and to grow often. Plants live to grow, and Earth's food deserts are counting on you!

Celebrate Your Garden!

You did it!

Author Bio

The Green Neighbor is Tina Johnson, an environmental justice and public health advocate and a lifelong resident of West Harlem, NYC. The Green Neighbor is committed to building sustainable communities through knowledge and action.

With her history of community engagement, health education, and environmental activism, her books aim to grow environmental understanding through accessible topics and practical activities.

Each book encourages readers to explore everyday actions that support local environments and promote stewardship.

The Green Neighbor believes small steps can lead to healthier, happier lives and a healthier planet.

Her goal is to spark curiosity and inspire sustainable change—one neighborhood, one garden, or one habit at a time.

www.ingramcontent.com/pod-product-compliance
Lightning Source LLC
Chambersburg PA
CBHW051628140626
46547CB00033B/2922